Newbridge Discovery Links®

RING of FIRE

Leonard Hort

Newbridge

A Haights Cross Communications Company

Ring of Fire
ISBN: 1-58273-723-1

Program Author: Dr. Brenda Parkes, Literacy Expert
Content Reviewer: John Ewert, Geologist and member of
   Volcano Disaster Assistance Program (VDAP)
Teacher Reviewer: Carmen Alvarez-Rodriguez, Austin ISD, Austin, TX

Written by Leonard Hort
Editorial and Design Assistance by Curriculum Concepts

Newbridge Educational Publishing
11 East 26th Street, New York, NY 10010
www.newbridgeonline.com

Cover Photograph: A Galápagos volcano erupting
Table of Contents Photograph: Galápagos wildlife

Photo Credits
Cover: Tui De Roy/Minden Pictures; Contents page: Tui De Roy/Minden Pictures; pages 4–5: Dave
Harlow/U.S. Department of the Interior, U.S. Geological Survey, David A. Johnston Cascades Volcano
Observatory, Vancouver, Washington; page 9: Stephen & Donna O'Mera/Photo Researchers, Inc.; page 10:
Liaison Agency, Inc.; page 11: Bob Krist/CORBIS; pages 12–13: Mark Moffett/Minden Pictures; page 13:
(top) Tim Davis/Photo Researchers, Inc., (bottom) Michael T. Sedam/CORBIS; page 14: Tui De Roy/
Minden Pictures; page 15: (top) Christian Grzimek/OKAPIA/Photo Researchers, Inc., (bottom) Frans
Lanting/Minden Pictures; page 16: (background) Soames Summerhays/Photo Researchers, Inc., (inset)
Bernhard Edmaier/SPL/Photo Researchers, Inc.; pages 18–19: Bettmann/CORBIS; pages 20–21: Christie's
Images/CORBIS; page 21: Bettmann/CORBIS; page 22: Ralph White/CORBIS; page 23: Francolon
Guichard/Liaison Agency, Inc.; page 24: David A. Hardy/SPL/Photo Researchers, Inc.; page 25: Peter
Ryan/SCRIPPS/SPL/Photo Researchers, Inc.; page 26: Michael S. Yamashita/CORBIS; page 27: (top)
Jeffry W. Myers/CORBIS, (center) Macduff Everton/CORBIS, (bottom) Pablo Corral/CORBIS; page 28:
U.S. Department of the Interior, U.S. Geological Survey, David A. Johnston Cascades Volcano Observatory,
Vancouver, Washington; page 29: C. Dan Miller, USGS/CVO/U.S. Department of the Interior, U.S.
Geological Survey, David A. Johnston Cascades Volcano Observatory, Vancouver, Washington; page 30:
©The Newark Museum/Art Resource, NY

Maps/Illustrations on pages 6–7, 8, 11, 17 by Steven Stankiewicz

10 9 8 7 6 5 4

TABLE OF CONTENTS

A SLEEPING GIANT AWAKENS

Mount Pinatubo in the Philippines had been a peaceful place for about 500 years. More than 20,000 people lived on its grassy slopes, farming the rich soil. But on April 2, 1991, ash and steam began to shoot out of **vents** in the mountain. The earth began to tremble. Then, on June 15, explosions blasted away the top 500 feet of the mountain. Clouds of ash shot up 25 miles high in the sky, and rocks the size of grapefruits rained down. The day grew as dark as night, and strange blue, green, and red colored lightning flashed. Then the earthquakes began. Mount Pinatubo, which had long been asleep, or dormant, had become an active **volcano**.

Mount Pinatubo's explosion was one of the most powerful in 100 years.

What caused Mount Pinatubo to blow its top? For ages, the fearsome power of volcanoes remained a mystery. People noticed that there were volcanoes all around the Pacific Ocean. They called this the **Ring of Fire**, but they could not explain it. Scientists wondered why the Ring of Fire was plagued by earthquakes, too. Recently they began to answer these questions.

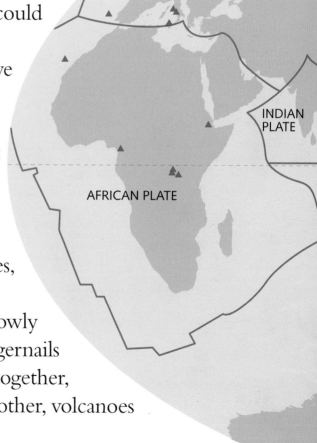

Have you ever looked at a globe and seen how the continents could almost fit together like a giant jigsaw puzzle? Scientists believe that when the first dinosaurs appeared, all of Earth's land was part of one supercontinent called **Pangaea**. Slowly, over millions of years, Pangaea broke apart into giant chunks called **plates**. These land plates, along with great ocean floor plates, move around or drift slowly at about the rate that your fingernails grow. Where the plates push together, pull apart, or slide past one another, volcanoes and earthquakes can occur.

EURASIAN PLATE

INDIAN PLATE

AFRICAN PLATE

PLATES ON THE MOVE

The Pacific and Eurasian plates are crashing into each other at a rate of a few inches every year.

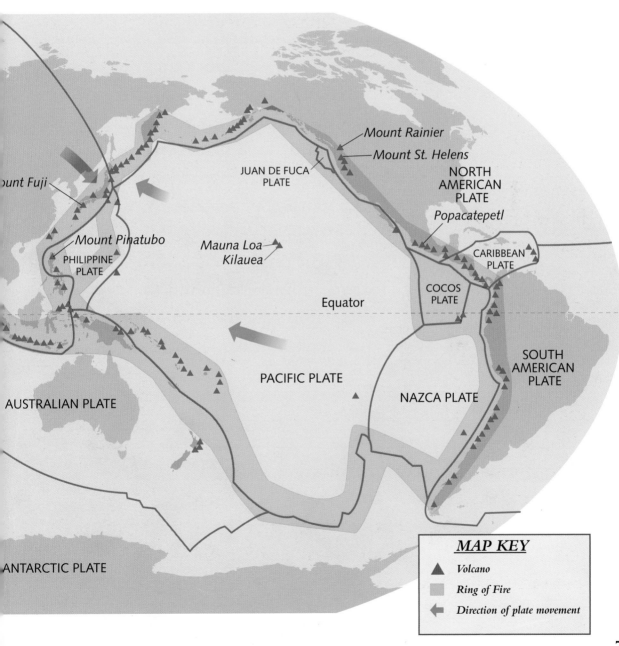

Mount Rainier

Mount St. Helens

JUAN DE FUCA PLATE

NORTH AMERICAN PLATE

Popacatepetl

ount Fuji

Mount Pinatubo

PHILIPPINE PLATE

Mauna Loa
Kilauea

CARIBBEAN PLATE

COCOS PLATE

Equator

AUSTRALIAN PLATE

PACIFIC PLATE

NAZCA PLATE

SOUTH AMERICAN PLATE

ANTARCTIC PLATE

MAP KEY

▲ Volcano

■ Ring of Fire

← Direction of plate movement

VOLCANOES

ach volcano is different, but they all begin deep below **Earth's crust**, or outer layer, where huge blobs of melted rock called **magma** rise toward the surface. On the Ring of Fire, volcanoes form because, as the Pacific plate crashes or pushes under other plates, magma builds up. Filled with gases, hot magma can act a bit like a can of soda that is opened after being shaken. It can explode. When the magma **erupts**, or reaches the surface through a vent, it is called **lava**. Over time, layers of lava form a mountain around the vent. Both the mountain and the vent are called a volcano.

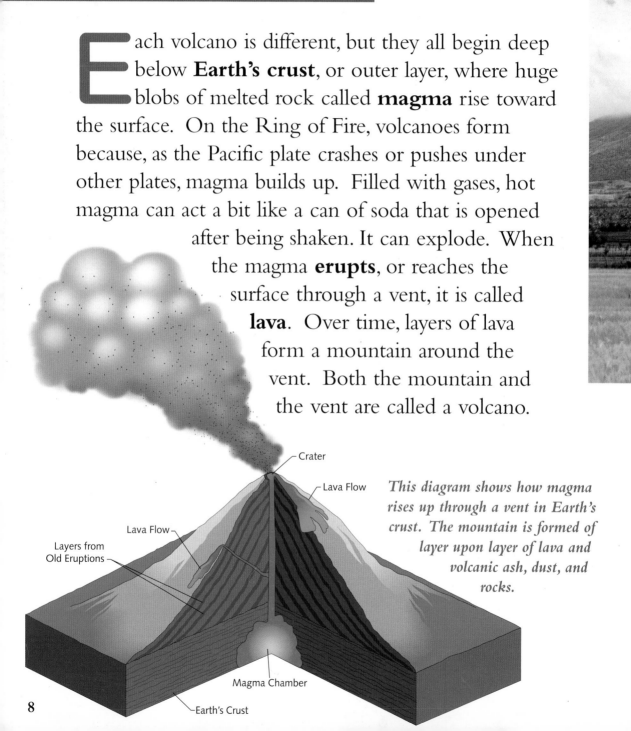

Crater

Lava Flow

Lava Flow

Layers from
Old Eruptions

Magma Chamber

Earth's Crust

This diagram shows how magma rises up through a vent in Earth's crust. The mountain is formed of layer upon layer of lava and volcanic ash, dust, and rocks.

Big, with sloping sides, Mount Mayon is a composite volcano.

Volcanoes come in lots of different shapes and sizes. Where runny lava oozes to the surface, giant mound-shaped mountains form. They are called shield volcanoes. When mostly bits of rock called **tephra** explode from a vent, volcanoes shaped like upside-down ice cream cones form. Called cinder cones, they form smaller mountains. The big, beautiful volcanoes that you often see in pictures are called composite volcanoes. They are built up as explosive eruptions of tephra and flows of lava pile up in layers.

Falling ash turns day into night.

What happens after a volcano erupts? At Mount Pinatubo, mud slides buried fields and villages, while thick blankets of falling ash closed schools, roads, and airports over much of the country. Winds spread ash and gases around the world. This created spectacular pink sunsets, but it also lowered Earth's average temperature for several years. As many as 800 people died at Mount Pinatubo. The homes of around 50,000 more people were buried, burned, or destroyed.

Hundreds of thousands of acres of farmland became a wasteland of volcanic ash and dust. Yet the catastrophe could have been far worse if 80,000 people had not listened to warnings and evacuated the area before it was too late.

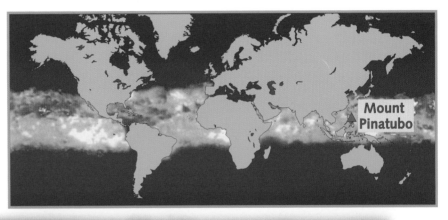

In two months, ash from Mount Pinatubo traveled all the way around the world, forming a band in the air around the planet. Sunsets were colored a "Pinatubo pink."

Plants and animals returned to Mount St. Helens in Washington State not long after the mountain blew its top in 1980.

For all their danger and destructive power, volcanoes are an important creative force in our world. Billions of years ago, volcanoes brought Earth's air and water to the surface. Undersea and coastal volcanoes

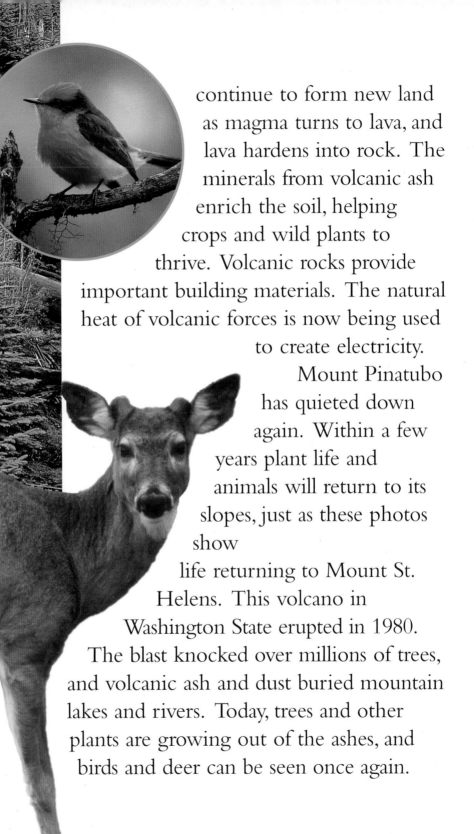

continue to form new land as magma turns to lava, and lava hardens into rock. The minerals from volcanic ash enrich the soil, helping crops and wild plants to thrive. Volcanic rocks provide important building materials. The natural heat of volcanic forces is now being used to create electricity.

Mount Pinatubo has quieted down again. Within a few years plant life and animals will return to its slopes, just as these photos show

life returning to Mount St. Helens. This volcano in Washington State erupted in 1980. The blast knocked over millions of trees, and volcanic ash and dust buried mountain lakes and rivers. Today, trees and other plants are growing out of the ashes, and birds and deer can be seen once again.

RIFTS AND HOT SPOTS

Just as plates can move together, they can also drift apart, forming a **rift**, a crack in Earth's crust. Whether this happens under the sea or on land, magma will usually rise to the surface as lava, then cool to form new crust. Undersea volcanoes can grow and grow until they rise above the water as islands. The Galápagos Islands off the coast of Ecuador in South America were formed this way.

The isolation of the islands, and the richness of the waters around them, have made the Galápagos home to

Unknown anywhere else in the world, marine iguanas crowd the Galápagos coastline.

many unique species—500-pound tortoises; marine iguanas that swim in the ocean to feed on algae; and a strange group of birds, including the rare flightless cormorant and penguins that never see ice.

This giant prickly pear cactus provides food for the huge Galápagos tortoise. On a diet of cactus and other native plants, tortoises can live for more than 200 years.

The magma that wells up to form the Hawaiian Islands
is runnier than most. It can flow as quickly as 35 miles
an hour, melting or burning everything in its path.

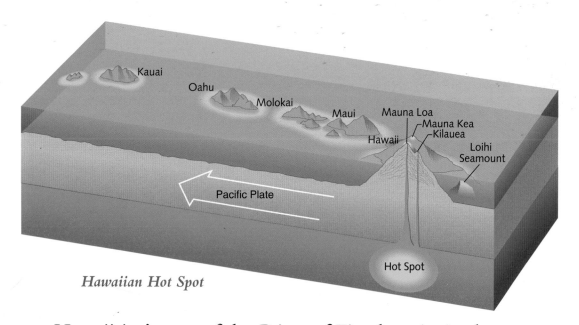

Hawaiian Hot Spot

Hawaii isn't part of the Ring of Fire, but sits in the middle of it. Look at the diagram above. Deep beneath the Pacific Ocean floor, a thick column of hot magma has been rising up for tens of millions of years. As the Pacific plate moves slowly over this **hot spot**, oozing lava has formed at least 82 volcanoes in a long string known as the Hawaiian Islands. The volcanoes farthest from the hot spot are the oldest, and extinct. The Big Island of Hawaii now sits over the hot spot, causing lava to flow from both Mauna Loa and Kilauea.

Loihi, the youngest Hawaiian volcano, has been steadily building up on the seafloor southeast of the big island. It could burst through the ocean's surface to start a new island paradise 10,000 to 60,000 years from now. Meanwhile, as the enormous Pacific plate creeps to the northwest, what do you think can happen at its edges where it rubs against its neighbors?

FAULTS AND EARTHQUAKES

One of the biggest earthquakes of the last century occurred in Alaska on March 27, 1964. It began as a gentle rocking of the earth. At first, people were not very concerned. They were used to small tremors. But this quake grew worse. The ground began to roll like ocean waves. The quake only lasted about five minutes, but entire blocks of houses were moved. Many buildings collapsed.

Earthquakes are most common along **faults**, cracks deep in Earth's crust, usually found where plates rub against one another. The Dinali fault near Anchorage and the well-known San Andreas fault in California formed because the Pacific plate is sliding past the North American plate at a rate of about two inches a year, but sometimes the plates become locked together.

Pressure builds . . . and builds . . . and builds until the plates break free from each other in an earthquake. Quakes rarely last more than a few seconds; that five-minute quake in Alaska was the longest one in recorded history.

It is falling buildings, more than the earth moving, that injures people during an earthquake, like this one in Anchorage, Alaska.

冨嶽三十六景 神奈川沖浪裏

北斎改為一筆

Undersea and coastal quakes can send gigantic waves called **tsunamis** all the way across the ocean at speeds of about 600 miles per hour. Tsunamis are also called tidal waves, though they have nothing to do with the tides. A tsunami is almost unnoticeable as it travels across the deep sea, but it can hit the shore thousands of miles away with a series of waves as much as 100 feet high, often causing more destruction than the earthquake itself. Tsunamis from the great Alaska quake of 1964 killed more than 100 people, not only in Alaska but in Oregon and California as well.

When waves from the Alaska quake hit Crescent City, California, buildings were destroyed, power was knocked out, and fires broke out.

AN UNDERSEA MYSTERY

Many people thought that every corner of the planet had been discovered and mapped, and that if someone wanted to explore someplace new, they would have to travel in a rocket ship far from Earth. But in 1977, a strange world was discovered. It was a dark place with no sunlight. Boiling black clouds of minerals spewed out of volcanic vents. Nearby were carpets of giant clams and great red worms. Where was this world? At a rift in the ocean floor, one and a half miles beneath the waves of the Pacific Ocean.

Scientists discovered this hidden world traveling in ALVIN, a submersible specially built to withstand the crushing pressure felt on the ocean floor.

These five-foot-long tube worms were never photographed or even seen before 1977.

ALVIN is equipped with all sorts of scientific equipment, including a remote-controlled arm for taking samples, and television lights and cameras.

People thought that all life on Earth got its energy from the sun. But there is no energy from the sun available in the freezing darkness of the ocean floor. The strange creatures that live here must get their energy from inside Earth.

This painting shows the black smokers and some of the creatures that live around them in an ecosystem very different from any other on Earth.

All along the deep ocean rifts where plates are pulling apart, water seeps down into cracks in Earth's crust. As the freezing ocean water sinks lower, it nears the rising blobs of magma found there, heats up, and becomes rich with minerals like iron and copper. Now boiling hot, the water erupts through vents as jets of scalding black mineral water. As soon as these jets hit the cold ocean water, the minerals harden, forming tall, weirdly shaped chimneys. They are called black smokers. Bacteria thrive in the warm, mineral-rich water around these chimneys. And the strange animals here thrive on the bacteria or each other.

Large blind crabs scamper over a bed of huge (one-foot-long) clams found around the smokers.

LIFE ON THE RING OF FIRE

People have always lived near volcanoes in order to farm the rich soil. They may not realize that these sleeping giants, which have been dormant for hundreds of years, can become active with little warning. With the world's population growing, at least half a billion people live in areas that could be threatened by volcanoes.

TOKYO

SEATTLE

MEXICO CITY

QUITO

27

Nothing anyone can do can stop a volcano from erupting. But **volcanologists**, scientists who study volcanoes, have found ways to save thousands of lives. The Volcano Disaster Assistance Program (known as VDAP) is an international volcano quick-response team sponsored by the U.S. government. VDAP helps other countries to monitor volcanic activity. The team also prepares people for disaster by teaching them about the dangers, predicting when eruptions may occur, and

Always ready, this VDAP team rushes to another volcano.

showing how to get to safety in time. When two volcanoes destroyed most of the houses in Rabaul, Papua New Guinea, in 1994, only three people died, while about 30,000 were safely evacuated.

As scientists learn more about the Ring of Fire and its earthquakes and volcanoes, they are better able to predict these events.

A team installs equipment that will monitor any shaking or trembling of the earth—a sign that magma is rising.

As earthquakes and volcanoes continue to transform the landscape around the Ring of Fire, new islands form. Forests, lakes, and rivers, as well as farms and villages, are sometimes destroyed. But the land is made richer, and from the ashes new things grow. Then people return to farm the rich soil again. As people understand the dangers, life in this unique and beautiful region will be enjoyed more safely.

Fourteen-year-old Miho Suzuki lives in Japan near the volcano called Mount Fuji. Miho wrote this poem about it:

Behind Mt. Fuji
the setting sun
a fine tomorrow

Ando Hiroshige is known around the world for his paintings of Mount Fuji.

Glossary

Earth's crust: the cool outer layer of the planet

erupts: what a volcano does when magma flows or explodes through a vent to Earth's surface

faults: cracks deep inside Earth's crust, often found at the boundary between plates

hot spot: a place where a great blob of hot magma wells up under Earth's crust, often forming volcanoes

lava: melted rock that has reached Earth's surface

magma: hot melted rock found below the surface of the earth

Pangaea: the original landmass believed to have once included all of Earth's continents

plates: huge chunks of rock that carry Earth's ocean floor and the continents

rift: a crack in Earth's crust that is formed when plates drift apart

Ring of Fire: a zone of volcanoes and earthquakes that circles the Pacific plate, forming a great ring

tephra: magma that hardens into ash, dust, or rocks as big as boulders, before it reaches Earth's surface

tsunamis: gigantic ocean waves caused by undersea or coastal earthquakes or volcanoes. Tsunamis are often called tidal waves.

vents: openings in Earth's surface called volcanoes, where magma erupts

volcano: a vent in Earth's crust caused by molten rock forcing its way to the surface. Volcanoes may be active, dormant, or extinct. There are shield, cinder-cone, and composite volcanoes.

volcanologists: scientists who study volcanoes

Index

Websites

Find out more about volcanoes and earthquakes at
volcano.und.nodak.edu/
www.terraquest.com/galapagos/
volcanoes.usgs.gov/